ABCs OF HALLOWEEN

By Elizabeth Gauthier

St. Clair Shores, Michigan

1st Edition
Text © 2020 Elizabeth Gauthier
Images from Adobe Stock
All rights reserved. No part of this book may be reproduced or copied in any way without written consent of the publisher other than short quotations for articles or review.

For information about permissions
please write Gauthier Publications at:

Gauthier Publications
P.O. Box 806241
Saint Clair Shores, MI 48080
Attention: Permissions Department

Frog Legs Ink is an imprint of Gauthier Publications
www.FrogLegsInk.com

Proudly printed and bound in the USA

ISBN: 978-1-942314-59-2

Library of Congress information on file

To all those who love Halloween

Apple cider

Bb

Black cat

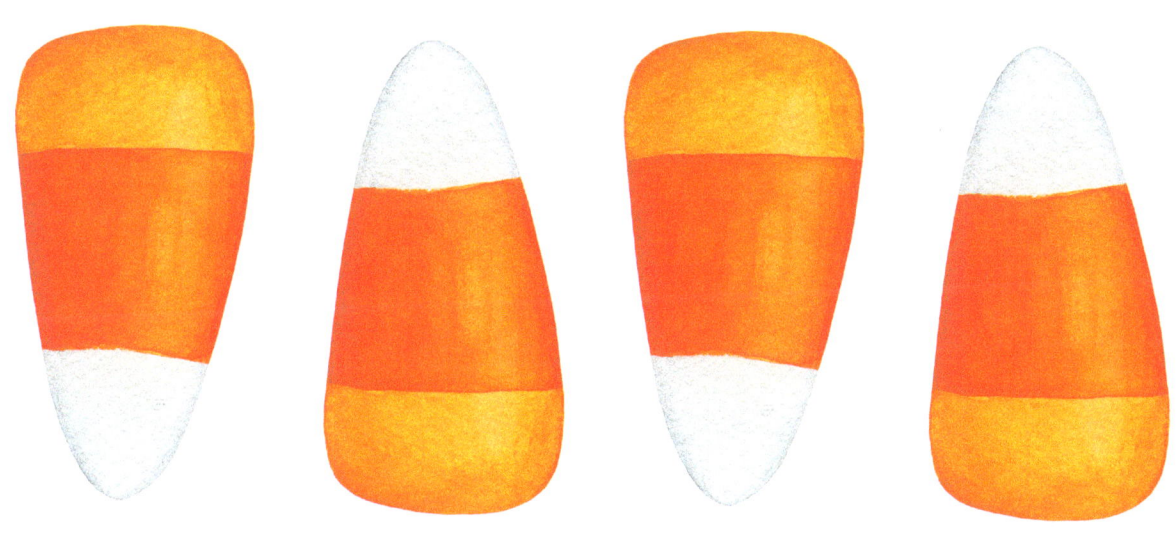

Candy corn

Dd

Decorations

Eyeballs

Frankenstein's

favorite foods

Hh

Haunted house

Illuminated houses

Jj

Jack-o-lantern

Kk

Knight

Ll

Lollipop

Mm

Mummy

Nighttime

October

Pumpkins

Raven

Ss

Spiderweb

Tarantula

Uu

Umbrella

Vampire

eXtra candy

Yy

Yellow moon

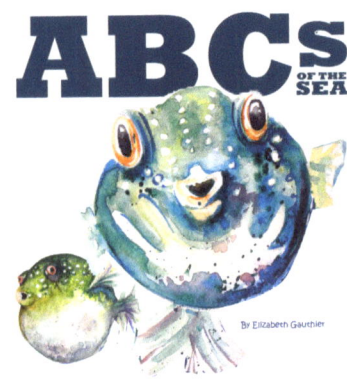

1 2 3 with me series
by Elizabeth Gauthier

Look for additional activities & lesson plans!

www.ingramcontent.com/pod-product-compliance
Lightning Source LLC
Chambersburg PA
CBHW040021050426
42452CB00002B/78